# Plant Partnerships

written by
## Joyce Pope

# Facts On File
*New York • Oxford • Sydney*

Published in the United States in 1990
by Facts On File, Inc., 460 Park Avenue South,
New York, NY 10016

**A Templar book**
Devised and produced by The Templar Company plc,
Pippbrook Mill, London Road, Dorking,
Surrey RH4 1JE, Great Britain

**Library of Congress Cataloging-in-Publication Data**

Pope, Joyce.
    Plant Partnerships / Joyce Pope.
       p.    cm. -- (Plant life)
    Includes bibliographical references.
    Summary: Surveys those plants which depend upon
animals or other plants for their habitat or survival.
    ISBN 0-8160-2422-7
    1. Botany--Ecology--Juvenile literature.    2.
Symbiosis--Juvenile literature.    3. Plants--Juvenile
literature.   [1. Symbiosis   2. Plants.]   I. Title.   II.
Series.
QK918.P67   1990
581.5'2482--dc20                              90-32395
                                                  CIP
                                                  AC

Facts On File books are available at special discounts
when purchased in bulk quantities for businesses,
associations, institutions or sales promotions. Please call
our Special Sales Department in New York at
212/683–2244 (dial 800/322–8755 except in NY, AK or HI).

*Notes to Readers*
There are some words in this book that are printed in
**bold** type. An explanation of them is given in the
glossary on page 58.

*Editor* Wendy Madgwick
*Designer* Mike Jolley
*Illustrator* Anne Savage

Color separations by Positive Colour Ltd, Maldon, Essex
Printed and bound by L.E.G.O., Vicenza, Italy

10 9 8 7 6 5 4 3 2 1

# Contents

# The Great Partnerships

The Planet Earth is a spaceship, in orbit around the sun. Until humans learned how to split atoms and take power from them, all of the energy used by almost every living thing came from the sun. Only a few strange, deep-sea creatures managed to survive without it.

There is one very important difference between plants and animals. This is not, as some people think, the fact that animals can move about freely, while plants are immobile. The thing that really separates plants from animals is that plants can use the sun's energy directly, while animals have to get it secondhand.

### Food from the air

Plants, growing in the light, can build up **sugars** and **starches** in their leaves using the green pigment **chlorophyll**. They combine carbon dioxide gas from the air and water from the soil by a process called **photosynthesis**. Other, more complex chemicals, such as proteins and oils, use **minerals** which the plants take from the soil or water in which they live.

### Food webs

Animals, unlike plants, cannot make their own food. They have to eat. This means that they take something alive, or which has been alive, and digest it, breaking it down into simpler chemicals. They can then build these into complicated animal cells. Many animals, such as caterpillars or cows, eat plants. Others, such as tarantulas or tigers, feed on flesh, but their **prey** is often a plant eater – or the eater of a plant eater. Minerals are removed from the soil by the plants and then eaten by the animals, but the minerals are returned to the soil via the animals' droppings and eventually their dead bodies.

As well as the great food partnership between all plants and animals, there are many small associations; plants with other plants, or plants with animals. This book is about some of those lesser partnerships.

*▼ The major difference between plants and animals is that plants can use energy direct from the sun to make food in their leaves. Animals cannot do this. They have to eat plants or the flesh of other animals.*

## THE GREAT PARTNERSHIPS

*A*nother *important partnership exists between all plants and animals. Each acts as a waste disposal unit for the other. Plants take carbon dioxide gas from the air and use it in photosynthesis to make sugars and starches. They use all the carbon but reject some of the oxygen as a waste product. Before there were plants, the earth's gases included little oxygen. Animals, which need oxygen to breathe, could not have survived in such an atmosphere. When animals breathe, they take in the oxygen that the plants provide and breathe out carbon dioxide, which is used by plants to make more sugars and starches.*

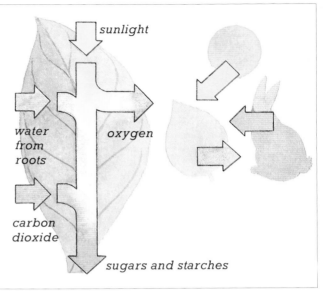

sunlight

water from roots

oxygen

carbon dioxide

sugars and starches

▲ *All animals depend on plants for their food. This does not sound like a good partnership, because animals seem to be the main winners. In fact, without animals plants would not grow so well.*

▶ *The two main kinds of living things are plants and animals. Both vary greatly in size, shape and color.*

# Plants Support Plants

**A**ll green plants must have light. They grow up and spread outward to catch all that they can of the sun's energy. They shadow the ground, but often smaller plants fight to get a share of the light by climbing over their bigger neighbors.

◄ *The stems of lianas hang loosely, for they must be able to move and sway with the forest trees. Some lianas measure more than 525 feet (160 meters), which is greater than the height of any tree. Liana stems are often flattened or lobed into odd shapes, which make them very strong and flexible.*

▼ *Plants use all sorts of ways to climb. Some use thorns or prickles; some have tendrils; some twine around other plants.*

Many climbing plants have thorns or prickles which help them to hang on to anything they touch. The weak stems of goosegrass are hooked with little prickles that enable it to scramble over stronger, woody plants. It also sticks to animals' fur or our clothes.

Plants like brambles and roses grow long arching stems. If they can find no support they make a compact bush, but they prefer to grow up and over trees using their thorns like climbing irons. They may make a dense thicket among the branches of their host and hold on so strongly that they will not be dislodged by even the most violent wind.

## Corkscrew tendrils

Tendrils are used by many kinds of climbing plants. These thread-like growths look like tight corkscrew curls. The tip of a tendril is very sensitive so if one touches something slightly rough, such as a twig, it bends in the direction of the twig and starts to curl around it. This may happen in less than a minute.

## Twining

Some other kinds of plants such as runner beans, hops or convolvulus do not have tendrils but the whole plant twines around a support. The growing tip of most twining plants takes about two hours to swing round in a circle. If it touches a suitable support it loops around and up. Some kinds of twining plants circle clockwise and some counterclockwise. All plants of the same kind turn in the same direction, but nobody knows why this should be.

## Giant climbers

The biggest of all the climbing plants are tropical lianas. They start life as shrubs, which carry tendrils or prickles on long shoots. At first the lianas use small trees for support, but they do not stop growing until they have reached the top-most **canopy** of the forest. Once in the light, they develop spreading **crowns** which may link several large trees together. Although the trunks of lianas are not as massive as the trunks of the forest giants, they are thick and strong enough to carry water and minerals from the forest floor up to the tops of the trees.

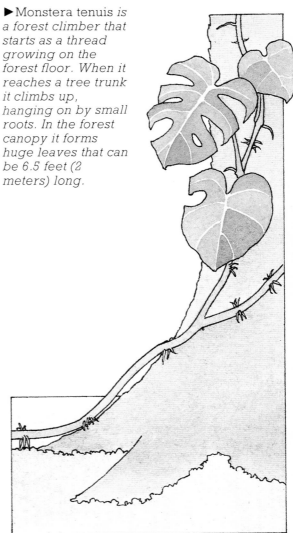

▶ *Monstera tenuis is a forest climber that starts as a thread growing on the forest floor. When it reaches a tree trunk it climbs up, hanging on by small roots. In the forest canopy it forms huge leaves that can be 6.5 feet (2 meters) long.*

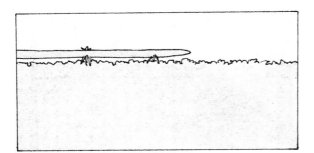

# Special Tendrils and Roots

**S**ome plants get protection and support from things that are too big to twine round or too smooth for thorns or prickles to hold on to. One way that they have solved the problems of upward growth is to have tendrils that shun the light.

▶*Ivy clings to rough surfaces by short roots. Sometimes it will prop up an old, decaying tree, and it adds to the richness of its **habitat** by giving protection to many small birds and insects.*

In some of the trumpet flowers the tendrils grow on the shaded side of the plant and push into the darkness of any crevice that they find. Once there, the tips swell, so that they hold very firmly. The plant is not held too rigidly because of the coiled spring shape of the tendril.

## Sticky tendrils

The Virginia creeper can climb up completely smooth surfaces, even glass. Each tendril has several tiny swellings which produce a sticky substance that glues the plant to the wall or tree that it is growing on. Each one can take a weight of about 2 lbs (1 kg).

## Clinging roots

Some plants use special roots to grip as they climb a tree or wall. Ivy, for instance, has short roots that grope and hold on to the roughness of bark or bricks. These roots are used only for holding on to its support. Ivy is not a parasite; it gets moisture and minerals from the soil and makes its own food by photosynthesis.

*▶ A single plant of Virginia creeper will have thousands of sticky tendrils. There is little chance of its being torn from its support. The tendrils live for one year, but the gluey discs remain. If you look closely at a wall that is covered with Virginia creeper you will see the brown remains of the discs where the vine clung to the wall in previous years.*

## DEADLY STRANGLERS

*Not all climbers are harmless. The strangler figs have earned their name by killing the trees that support them. A strangler fig starts to grow from a seed dropped by a bird. The seedling usually **germinates** in a place where dead leaves have made a little*

*humus in the crotch of a tree. To begin with, it develops slowly, but soon it produces a root. This may have to drop many feet before it reaches the ground, but once it has rooted the fig gets water and **nutrients** and grows much more quickly. It puts out more roots and these make a network that completely surrounds the trunk of the supporting tree. Eventually the upward growing part of the fig bursts through the topmost branches of its host and overshadows it. Deprived of light and also of water and minerals taken by the fig roots, the host tree is weakened and soon dies. Even after the tree has completely rotted away, the strangler fig continues to flourish. The fig's trunk is quite hollow inside, for it is made of a lattice of thick roots.*

# The Epiphytes

In their greed for light, some plants have abandoned their hold on the ground and use other plants to lift them towards the sun. They are known as **epiphytes,** a name that comes from the Greek words for "upon" and "plant." Most epiphytes are fairly small and use their hosts only for support. Epiphytes' roots (if any) are only used for hanging on to the host and for taking in water.

◄*In temperate forests of North America, draperies of* **mosses** *and* **club mosses** *hang from the trees. Sometimes they become so thick and heavy that they shade the trees and break their branches.* **Saprophytes** *get their food from rotting plants or animals. They are never found on living things.*

▲*Orchids usually have roots that can absorb rain water quickly, and their thick, waxy leaves can also hold and store water.*

The surface of the host plant is usually dry, so the leaves of epiphytes often have special methods of storing water. Some epiphytes get the minerals that they need for growth from dead leaves which have rotted to make humus. Others can manage on small amounts dissolved in rain or even from dust in the air.

## From seashore to forests

Epiphytes are found in most environments. Even on the seashore some seaweeds get support and shelter from the pounding waves by growing on larger weeds. But epiphytes grow most successfully in forests where there are many different habitats.

Near the ground and on the lower trunk, where there is not much light, tiny **algae** and mosses grow. Higher up, where the air is drier, **lichens** often thrive. In tropical forests the canopy of the trees is brilliant with flowering epiphytes. In cool regions of the world most of the epiphytes are non-flowering plants. The largest of these are **ferns** although most are the much smaller

mosses and lichens. Sometimes the trees grow special roots from their branches to take water and food from the epiphytes!

## Tropical delight

Mosses and ferns are found also in tropical forests. Some, such as the bird's nest fern, make hanging gardens with soil formed from dead leaves.

The most successful of the epiphytes are the orchids. About 9,000 different species or almost half of all known orchids are epiphytes. Another group of plants found in tropical forests are the bromeliads or tank plants. Their broad leaves grow tightly pressed together to make a tall cup which in some cases can hold over a gallon (5 liters) of water.

The bright flowers of many orchids and bromeliads attract **pollinators** – not only insects but also birds such as humming birds and sunbirds. If the flowers are not pollinated, they often last for a very long time. This is one reason why epiphytic orchids and bromeliads have become popular house plants.

◀*Bromeliads have special partnerships with many animals. The little ponds which they make in the tree tops are the homes of creatures found nowhere else. These include insects, snails and even frogs and salamanders.*

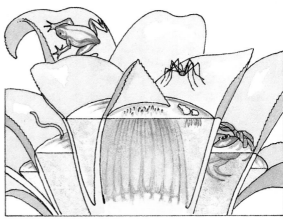

# Parasites

Although large plants are often festooned with others that cause them no damage, this is not always the case. In some associations one partner is a **parasite** and steals nutrients from the other, known as the **host**.

Perhaps the most famous of all plant parasites is the European mistletoe, which is found on various kinds of tree. It is only a partial parasite, for it has green leaves that make its food and it takes only support, water and minerals from its host. The fruit of the mistletoe is a berry, which is eaten by birds, particularly the mistle thrush. When the bird wipes its beak on a branch, it may leave the sticky seed glued to the bark. This seed soon germinates and grows a root that fixes it more firmly to the tree. Special roots called **haustoria** grow into the wood of the host tree and from them other roots develop and grow into the **xylem** tubes that carry water and minerals from the soil.

## Total parasites

Some parasites do not have green leaves, but rely entirely on their hosts for food and water. Many of these completely parasitic plants, for example the dodder, are specialists and attach themselves to only one kind of host or at best a few closely related species. In general, it is not in the interest of parasites to kill the hosts that provide them with a living, but sometimes they do. Some fungi like the honey fungus and many mildews may kill the plants from which they steal shelter and food.

▶ *The mistletoe has many relatives. One of the strangest is an Australian tree, sometimes known as the Christmas tree. It is unusual because it is partly parasitic on grasses and other plants that are very much smaller than itself.*

▲ *The word "parasite" often makes people think of something horrible. But broomrapes, which are completely parasitic, growing on the roots of their host plants, often have very beautiful flowers.*

▲ *Few plants grow in the dim light of the forest floor in Sumatra and Indonesia. But sometimes cabbage-sized buds can be found on the roots of trees. These open to show the bright colors of* Rafflesia arnoldi, *the biggest flower in the world, which can measure 3 feet (1 meter) across.*

◄ *The dodder looks like a mass of pink threads tangled over plants such as gorse or nettles. It has lost all contact with the ground, although its seeds germinate there. Its roots penetrate the stems of its hosts and it takes all that it needs from them.*

# Plants Depending on Plants

**S**ome plants live together in such a way that they both benefit from the association. Usually one of the partners is much larger, but if one of them dies, so does the other. This sort of relationship is called **symbiosis**, a name that comes from two Greek words and means "living together."

Many flowering plants, including orchids and some woodland trees such as oaks, beeches, pines and eucalypts, depend, particularly in the early stages of their life, on minute **fungi**. The fungi make a fine network of threads, called **mycorrhiza**, which completely surround the roots of the larger plant. Roots covered with a sheath of mycorrhiza grow better and branch more than those without, so the whole plant benefits from the presence of the fungus. When plants are taken from one part of the world to another, they often cannot grow in their new home. This is probably because they do not have the right fungus partners.

### Feeding each other

The heathers and their relatives often grow in places where the soil is very poor. It is almost certain that they are able to

make use of such habitats because they are helped by mycorrhizal fungi. Unlike the mycorrhiza of oaks and pines, the threads invade the heather's roots, supplying the nitrogen and phosphates which the heather needs for growth. The fungus gains by taking sugars, but never so much that the heather is seriously weakened.

Many orchids have mycorrhiza that invade their roots in the same sort of way (see below). The roots of the strange pinesap or yellow birdsnest are also covered with mycorrhiza. However, the fungus is unable to provide enough food for the plant's rapid growth in the summer. But, the fungus also has a mycorrhizal association with the roots of trees, and it has been discovered that the mycorrhiza takes food from the tree and passes it on to the birdsnest – acting as a carrier from one plant to the other.

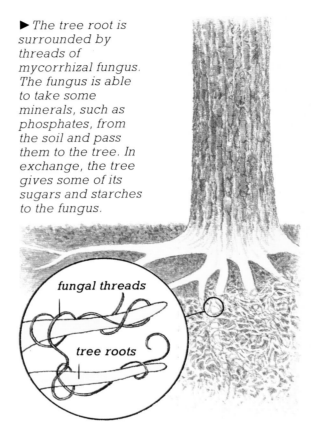

▶ *The tree root is surrounded by threads of mycorrhizal fungus. The fungus is able to take some minerals, such as phosphates, from the soil and pass them to the tree. In exchange, the tree gives some of its sugars and starches to the fungus.*

*fungal threads*

*tree roots*

◀ *The pinesap is a strange plant that grows in the dark northern forests of the world. It always* *has a thick layer of fungal threads that spread over its roots and those of nearby trees.*

## ORCHIDS AND FUNGI

*Orchids produce the smallest of all seeds, so tiny that there is not room for enough food for the new plant. Some orchid seeds germinate only when they are surrounded by the right sort of fungus. The fungus threads, which are able to use the humus in the soil for food, push into the newly germinated orchid seed. The seed then uses some of the fungus for its own growth. In due course the fungus takes some food from the orchid, but it is a see-saw affair, first one partner benefits, then the other.*

*orchid's roots*

*fungal threads*

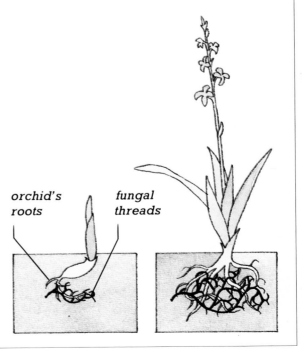

# Lichens

An oak tree can be recognized for what it is, and the mycorrhizal fungi around its root may also be identified. Although they grow together and benefit each other, each keeps its separate identity throughout its life. But things are different in a great group of plants called lichens.

There are about 18,000 different sorts of lichen. They are always formed of a large number of cells of a single-celled green plant called an alga and the fine threads of a fungus. When they grow together, they make plants that look nothing like either partner. They are often bigger and more complex and live longer than either partner could do alone.

## Living together

The fungus takes food that has been made in the light by the alga. In exchange, the fungus gives the alga a place where it can live without drying up, and perhaps helps it to obtain some of the minerals it needs for survival.

## Life in the cold

A lichen formed of an alga and a fungus is not only larger than the partners that form it, but is often able to survive in places that neither could live in on its own. Although they are found in most lowland habitats, including by the sea where they often make lines of green, yellow and black along the rocks, lichens are most noticeable in rocky places, in high mountains and in the Arctic. They are found at far greater heights than any other plants. They sometimes form so thin a crust on the rock that they look like part of it, and not like anything alive at all. The lichens produce acid that helps to break down the rocks to make the first soil in which other, larger plants can grow.

Lichens are among the slowest growing plants. A large tuft may be over 100 years old.

## HOW LICHENS SPREAD

*Lichens reach remote regions by means of **soredia**. These are made of a huge number of tiny grains, each as fine as dust, and they give a powdery look to the lichen. Each grain is made of a few cells of the alga wrapped around with threads of the fungus. The wind may carry these minute objects for long distances. Only a few survive, but so many are formed that some are bound to reach a suitable spot for living, often far away from their original home.*

►*Lichens come in many shapes and sizes, but there are three main types. There are those that are shrubby or tufted in appearance, others that are flat and lobed and look like leaves, and a third type that looks like a crust on the surface of rocks or stonework.*

*crusty lichen*

**shrubby lichen**

**leafy lichen**

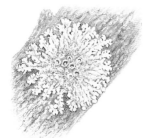

▼*In a lichen the green cells of the alga make a thin layer on the surface, where they can catch the light.*

*Other algal cells may be scattered among the threads of the fungus that compose most of the body of the lichen.*

*fungal threads*      *algal cells*

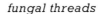

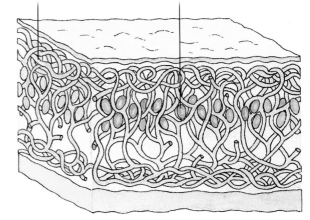

◄*Some lichens can be very large, like this* Usnea *from North America and Europe. Lichens grow very slowly and are very long-* *lived. They are rarely seen in towns, for most of them cannot tolerate pollution. They can only thrive in clean air.*

# Plant and Animal Partners

**A**lthough all plants and animals depend on each other in a general way, there are some creatures that live together in a symbiosis as close as that of the two sorts of plants in a lichen. The best known of these are the reef-building corals.

Reef-building corals live in shallow, clear, warm seas, because their soft tissues are crammed with minute plants of a kind found only in warm waters. The plants, which are known as **zooxanthellae**, are so tiny that 470,000 of them may exist in a cubic inch of a coral. Although they do not have leaves or flowers, they make their food in the same way as all plants and to do this they must have light. This is why

living, growing coral reefs are always in shallow waters lit by the sun.

## Chalky skeleton

When the plants use carbon dioxide to make sugars, some of the carbon is left over in the form of a carbonate. The coral combines this with calcium from the seawater to make a hard, chalky material. This makes up the coral's supporting skeleton. Corals can increase the size of their skeletons 14 times faster in sunlight, where the plants are active, than in the dark. A coral kept in the dark loses most of its zooxanthellae and slowly shrinks in size. Eventually it will die.

## Giant clams

Giant clams found in many coral reefs, are also home to zooxanthellae. The advantage to the plants is probably that they have a safe living place and a supply of the animal's waste products to convert into food. Some of this is returned quickly to the host animal, which feeds in part on tiny plants. It is difficult to prove how much help the giant clams get from their guests as only seven kinds of clams use plants in this way. They are all very big compared to other shells, so it is likely that their symbiosis with plants is the reason for their success.

◀ *Reef-building corals live only in shallow, clear, warm seas. The outer part of the reef may plunge to great depths, but this is formed of long-dead corals crowned with the living reef. Other kinds of corals, which do not make reefs, may live in deep, dark water.*

▲ *Some sea anemones like this* Anemonia sulcata *also have zooxanthellae. They give the anemone a green color in bright sunlight.*

▼ *Scientists still do not fully understand the way that corals and zooxanthellae live together, but it seems that each organism uses the other as a refuse collector. The plants give off oxygen as a waste product and this is used by the coral to breathe. The waste product of the coral is carbon dioxide. The plant takes this to make sugar for itself, and some sugar is "leaked" to the coral.*

# Sloths and Other Gardeners

In most partnerships between plants and animals each exists separately from the other. This is probably because most animals keep clean by grooming themselves and this removes any seeds or spores. However, a very few slow moving and inactive creatures allow, or even encourage, small plants to grow on them. These animals are sometimes called "gardeners."

Some insect gardeners are found in upland rain forests in New Guinea. These are flightless beetles, mainly weevils, whose shapes are masked by bumps and pits and grooves. Their disguise is improved still further by a number of small plants that grow in the furrows or grooves on their backs and the upper parts of their legs. These plants include fungi, algae, lichens and some kinds of mosses and **liverworts**. As well as offering the plants a place to live, the beetles

encourage them with a waxy secretion, which may give the plants the minerals that they need for growth. The beetles are unusually long-lived. The adults seem to survive for at least five years, so that the plants have time to grow fully.

## Farmer crabs

Other gardeners are found in shallow seas. These are spider crabs which, like the beetles, are slow moving and spiny. Many spider crabs attach bits of seaweeds to themselves. As with the sloths and the beetles, the weeds help to camouflage the crabs. But in some cases the crabs also use them as food. In this partnership the gardeners have become farmers!

◄Spider crabs plant seaweed on their backs. Sometimes the seaweed grows better on the backs of crabs than anywhere else. Perhaps this is because the waste products of the crabs make easy food for the plants.

▼In the miniature forests on their backs, some weevils from New Guinea carry plant-eating mites, threadworms and wheel animals. Some of these creatures have never been discovered anywhere else.

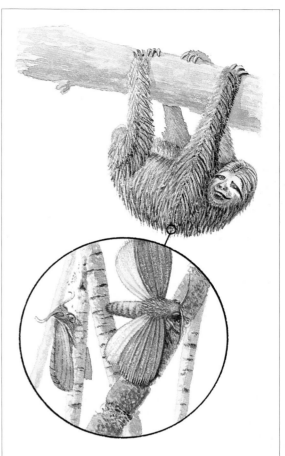

## SLOW-MOTION SLOTHS

*T*he sloths, which live in the tropical rain forests of South America, are the only mammals among the "gardeners." Sloths are the least active of all mammals. The three-toed sloth may remain in the same tree for long periods and seldom moves more than 130 feet (40 meters) in a day. When dry, the long fur of the sloths is gray, but most of the time it looks green. The reason for this is that the outer hairs are thick and spongy, with deep cracks or grooves in the surface. These make a living place for at least six different sorts of fine thread-like algae.

Most wild animals carry a number of other creatures in their fur. Sloths are unusual in that these include small moths and beetles. A single sloth may have more than 120 moths in its fur. These do not feed on the algae, but lay their eggs in the sloth's droppings.

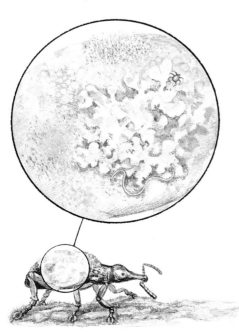

# Flowers and Pollination

The fossils of some of the earliest land plants, which date back about 400 million years, show marks of where they were nibbled by insects. Since those days plants and insects have existed alongside each other. Over the ages both have changed, often developing special partnerships.

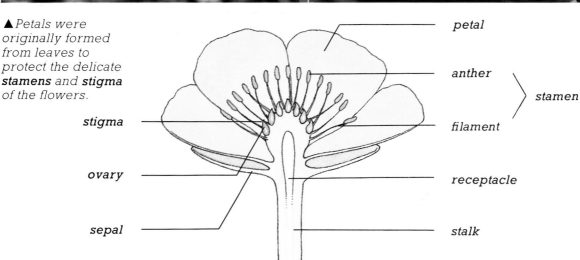

▲ *Petals were originally formed from leaves to protect the delicate* **stamens** *and* **stigma** *of the flowers.*

petal

anther

filament

stigma

ovary

sepal

receptacle

stalk

stamen

By far the most important partnership is that between flowers and the insects that pollinate them. **Pollination**, the spread of pollen from the male **anther** to the female **stigma**, must take place if the plant is to produce any seeds. A few kinds of plant are **self-pollinated**, but as a rule this leads to poor seeds and weak plants in the next generation. It is better if pollen is taken from one flower to another. Sometimes the wind carries pollen, but more often some kind of animal does the job. As insects can fly between one blossom and the next, they are the most suitable for the work. In a few cases, birds and mammals are the pollinators.

## The first pollinators

The first plants did not have flowers. They gave rise to the next generation by special cells called **spores**. These minute, wax-covered grains made good food for many primitive insects. The first plants with flowers lived about 120 million years ago. They had a great deal of pollen and insects would certainly have found this a useful source of food.

At that time there were no butterflies, bees or flies, so it is likely that beetles were the pioneers of pollination. As they went from one plant to another, they carried some of the pollen which had got stuck to them and left it in the next flower that they visited. This led to pollination and was so valuable a service that flowers slowly developed many ways to attract beetles and other insects.

## Petal power

Insects visiting flowers in search of food found that petals made a good landing and feeding place. Flowers with broad petals tended to be most successfully pollinated and their seeds would make more plants with broad petals. Plants with small petals were less often visited by insects and tended to die out.

Pollinating insects have good color vision and they are attracted to patches of different colors among the green of the leaves. In many instances petals became brightly colored. But insects cannot, on the whole, see pure red; it looks black to them. So, very few red flowers are pollinated by insects. Those, like poppies that look red to us, also have a color called ultraviolet, which insects can see, but which we cannot.

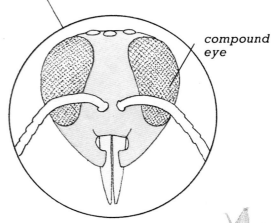

*▼Insect eyes are made of many separate lenses. They are not good at observing detail, but they can detect movement very easily. Most wild flowers have very thin stems, so that they sway in the slightest breeze. Very many flowers are star-shaped, or look star-shaped to insects, and this exaggerates the movement to the insects' eyes.*

*compound eye*

*Flowers that look plain to us appear patterned to insects.*

# Insect Pollinators

**T**he first insects were creatures that hatched from an egg. They looked like small versions of their parents. As they fed they molted and grew larger, but there was no break in their growth and they looked much the same throughout their lives.

▲*Bees have a special method of collecting pollen. They brush the sticky grains from their bodies into "pollen baskets" that are formed on their hind legs. You can easily see the pollen baskets when they are full of yellow pollen.*

◄*Often nectar is hidden in special tube-shaped petals, and only insects with long tongues, like bees, butterflies or moths, can reach it.*

The beetles and the other insect groups that developed later on had a different life pattern. The tiny creatures that hatch from their eggs are grubs, quite different in appearance from the adults. Most grubs have poor senses and cannot move much. They have one job in life and that is to feed and grow as quickly as possible.

## Sweet reward

The adults are active and have good senses, for they have the job of finding a mate and laying eggs. They do not grow or replace cells so they do not need to eat so much as the grubs. But most need some nourishment to give them energy. The best sort of food to do this is sugar, and many flowering plants produce sugary **nectar** to attract insects.

Often the nectar or the petals smell strongly and the insects are attracted by this, as well as the color and shape of the flower. As they search for the nectar, they get pollen on themselves and carry it to the next blossom that they visit. Nectar is provided by the plant as a "reward" for carrying out the task of pollination.

## Sticky pollen and hairy insects

Pollen that is blown by the wind is dry and powdery. Plants that rely on insects for pollination produce pollen that is sticky and clumps together easily, so that it clings to the insects. Good pollinators usually have hairy bodies so that they can collect a lot of pollen easily.

◄ *Sometimes, as in thoroughwax, the nectar is provided in shallow cups on the surface of the flower. Short-tongued insects, such as flies, are the pollinators of these blooms.*

## SIGNPOSTS TO SWEETNESS

*F lower petals are often colored with bright patches or lines which lead towards the center of the flower where the nectar is. These are called **honey guides**. Experiments have shown that when bees visit artificial flowers, with honey guides pointing towards the edges of the petals, they will follow the guides in the wrong direction and fall off! In nature the guides always lead the insects towards the sweet nectar.*

*A pattern of lines, which often form a star shape, lead the insect into the center of the flower.*

*Patterns of blotches and spots can also act as nectar guides.*

# Insect Partners

Some flowers that live in cool places attract insects by their warmth. Many plants of high mountains grow in a dense cushion shape, the stems forming a refuge for insects against the cold and high winds. When the weather becomes warmer and the plant is in flower, the insects leave their hiding places and find food nearby, pollinating the flowers as they do so.

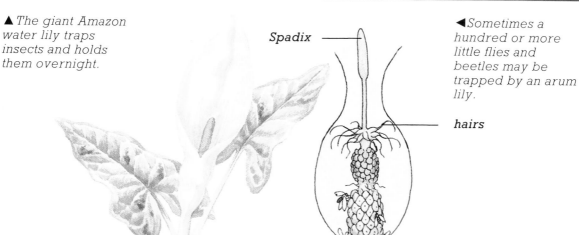

▲ *The giant Amazon water lily traps insects and holds them overnight.*

*Spadix*

◀*Sometimes a hundred or more little flies and beetles may be trapped by an arum lily.*

*hairs*

Some flowers, such as the mountain avens, turn their cup of petals towards the sun. They hold the heat and may be several degrees warmer than the cold air outside. Insects attracted by the flower linger in the warmth, taking plenty of time to get covered with pollen.

## Flower traps

Other kinds of flowers not only attract pollinators, but trap them and keep them prisoner until they have done their task. The giant Amazon water lily opens in the evening, and attracts beetles by its heavy scent. As night draws on, the flower closes, and it does not open again until the next evening. The trapped beetles feed on parts of the flower, and when they leave they carry pollen to another lily.

Arum lilies also trap insects. The shiny leaf-like **bract** or spathe that protects the tiny flowers at its base forms a sort of vertical skating rink, where insects can find no foothold. They slide down, but their way of escape is barred by stiff, downwardly pointing hairs. They wander about, and if they are carrying pollen from another flower they transfer it to the stigmas of the female parts of the arum, which rewards them with a drop of sticky liquid. After about 24 hours, the stiff hairs relax and the insects are freed. But as they leave they are showered with pollen from the stamens which they have to pass.

*▲ In the deserts of North America, Yucca flowers are pollinated by moths. After mating, the female collects pollen from the flowers. She works this into a ball which she carries to another plant. She lays her eggs near the **ovary** of the flower where the seeds will form. She then puts some of the pollen on the stigma, so that the plant will be pollinated and form seeds. When the caterpillars hatch, they eat some of the seeds, but leave plenty to make the next generation of Yucca.*

## "GALL FLOWERS"

*Some plants depend on a particular sort of insect for pollination. Some kinds of figs rely on a small wasp that lays its eggs in the flowers, where they make **galls**. But there are two sorts of flowers. Some plants have "gall flowers" and others have fertile flowers. The fig wasps visit both types of flower, carrying pollen from one to the other, but the wasps' eggs can only hatch and grow in the gall flowers. After pollination, the fertile flowers ripen to give edible figs.*

# The Orchid Specialists

**T**he orchid family contains more species than any other group of plants. Some orchid flowers are quite small but they all have a petal, called the lip petal, which is larger than the others and is often brightly colored or strangely shaped. It may be enlarged to form a sort of bag, or it may be drawn out into fantastic tails, but its job is always to attract pollinators.

Orchids usually contain nectar, often in a long tube called the spur formed at the back of the lip petal. Many orchids have a partnership with one kind of insect, which is the only one that can reach its nectar. Orchid flowers are often shaped so that insects reach nectar and pollen one way, but have to leave the flower by another route. This makes certain that pollination will take place.

## Pollinia

Some orchids use strange methods for sticking **pollinia** to their insect guests. In some tropical orchids the lip petal is pivoted and tips small insects, usually flies, against the part of the flower where a pollinium will be attached to it. Once the insect has gone, the lip swings back into position to repeat the movement with the next visitor.

## The right partner

In a particular area, many similar orchids may be in bloom at the same time. There seem to be two ways to prevent the wastage of cross pollination. One is that each orchid has its own pollinating species of insect, which is not attracted to any other kind of flower. The other is that each kind of orchid places its pollinia on a different part of the insect's body. For instance, a pollinium on the head will not be in the right place to pollinate a flower that sticks its pollen on to the thorax or abdomen. Some butterflies and moths collect pollinia on their long tongues!

▲ *The pollen of most orchids is different from that of other plants. As a rule, thousands of grains clump together to form pollinia. The pollinia get stuck to the insects that visit the orchid's flowers.*

▲ Some of the strangest orchids are those that drug bees with liquids or heavily scented chemicals. A dozy bee may take a long time to escape from the flower, and in doing so is certain to get pollinia stuck to its body. Once a bee has removed a pollinium, the flower often loses its scent for some hours, so that the same bee will not be tempted back. This prevents self-pollination.

▲ The lady's slipper orchid attracts small wild bees which enter the ''slipper'' of the lip petal by the large and obvious entrance. They cannot get out the same way, for the sides of the lip are glassy smooth, so they squeeze through a small exit near the back of the flower. As the bee makes its final escape, sticky pollen is attached to the hairs of its back.

# Orchids that Imitate Insects

**S**ome insects treat flowers like other insects. For instance, a kind of small bee often rests near *Oncidium* orchids in the forests of tropical America. These bees are territorial, and defend an area against others of their own kind. When the orchids stir in the wind, the bees behave as if their home space were being invaded. They fly at the flowers and try to knock them away. As a result of this, the orchid flowers are quickly pollinated.

◀*Small bees that live next to* Oncidium *orchids treat the flowers as if they were other bees. The flowers are pollinated in the rough and tumble.*

▶ *The mirror orchid is one of the most striking of the insect imitators. The center of the lip is a shimmering blue, and the edges are bordered with a fringe of reddish brown hairs.*

Some people think that the movement of these flowers looks like the flight of a female to the defending bee, and the buffeting is part of his courtship. Certainly there are bees in other parts of the world whose mating displays involve a similar kind of behavior.

## A mate or not?

The partnership between some kinds of orchids and their insect pollinators is so close that the plants both look and smell like the insects that they hope to attract. Other kinds of insects rarely visit these orchids and would get no reward, for they produce no nectar and their pollinia are placed where only the right kind of pollinator can collect them. These insect imitators attract the males of various kinds of bees, wasps and flies.

## Mirror orchids

The mirror orchid is partnered by a kind of wasp which has a fringe of long red hairs around the abdomen. Only the males visit the mirror orchid. They are probably attracted by its scent, and will seek it out even if it has been hidden. The females spend much of their time underground hunting for worms which they use as food for their grubs. They ignore the orchids completely, although they feed from other sorts of flowers.

It is likely that a male sees the blue part of the lip of the orchid as being like the wings of a female. He flies to it but makes no attempt to feed. Instead he tries to mate with it. The pollinia get stuck to the wasp's head and later they are transferred to another orchid when the wasp attempts to mate with it.

◀ *The bee orchid is an oddity among the insect imitators. It is visited by several sorts of insects, but they are rarely effective pollinators. After a certain length of time the filament that supports the pollinia wilts and the pollen swings down to the stigma. In spite of its appearance, the bee orchid seems to be self-pollinated.*

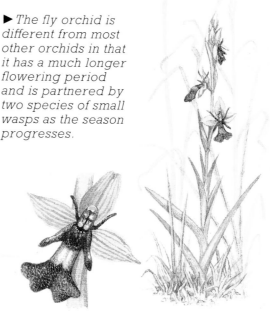

▶ *The fly orchid is different from most other orchids in that it has a much longer flowering period and is partnered by two species of small wasps as the season progresses.*

# Bird Pollinators

In the tropics some plants have a pollination partnership with birds rather than insects. As with insects, the birds take nectar and at the same time become smeared with pollen which they transfer to another plant. Birds that feed on nectar include hummingbirds in the Americas, sunbirds in Africa and India, and small parrots in Australia and nearby islands.

In all cases the birds need other food in addition to nectar and many also eat small insects. It may be that nectar-feeding developed in birds as they searched for insects amongst the flowers. A few insect-eating birds, such as warblers, have been seen sipping nectar, though they probably never act as pollinators.

## Tough, bright flowers

Most flowers pollinated by birds are toughly built, for birds are generally much more powerful than insects. Their beaks tend to damage the flowers, so these are usually protected with a thick **calyx** or bracts which often give the bird

◄ *Many humming-birds have beaks and tongues that exactly fit the size and shape of the nectar tubes of their particular flowers. The sword-billed hummingbird visits trumpet-shaped flowers with extremely long tubes. Often its beak is longer than its own body.*

## SPECIALIST FEEDERS

*T*he beaks and tongues of humming birds have to be very long to reach the nectar deep inside the flowers. Their tongues are usually brush-like at the tip, for gathering nectar, and rolled in at the sides to form a tube. A feeding humming bird shoots its tongue into the flower and then pulls it back into its mouth.

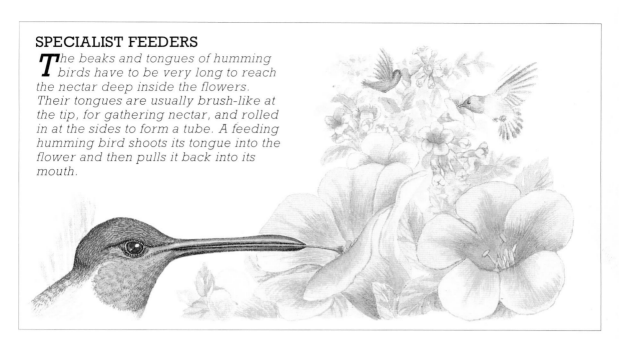

something to perch on as it searches for food. Most flowers that are pollinated by birds have their ovaries below the petals, so that the delicate parts where the seeds will develop remain unharmed by probing beaks or clutching claws. Parrots are very destructive, crushing the flowers with their beaks and claws in their eagerness to get at the nectar.

Many bird-pollinated flowers are red in color, or have petals that contrast strongly with the shade of the leaves. They do not have any scent because, unlike insects, most birds have no sense of smell. Flowers that attract birds usually make lots of nectar, but it is weaker than the nectar produced for insects. Nectar for birds has few nutrients other than sugar.

Many nectar-feeding birds migrate to follow the plants that can give them food. Hummingbirds in western North America leave the plains and fly high up into the mountains where the flowers that they need bloom later. They seem to remember from one season to the next where their food plants are to be found. Where the flowers are in masses hummingbirds defend the territory where they feed. Hummingbirds that feed on more widely spaced flowers do not do this.

▼ *Sunbirds live in Africa and Asia. Like humming-birds, they have long beaks and long, tubular tongues.*

▲ *The nectar-feeding parrots follow the* Eucalyptus *in bloom. They may also feed on soft fruit, making them unpopular with orchard owners.*

# Mammal Pollinators

**I**t is likely that many kinds of mammals become pollination partners of plants as they accidentally transfer pollen from one flower to another. In a few cases we can see how true partnerships may begin.

For instance, a plant called *Freycinetia*, which grows in Hawaii, is usually pollinated by birds. However, in recent years rats, which have been introduced into the island, have been attracted by the sugary bracts around the flower. The rats spread the pollen as they climb from one flower to another to feed.

## Honey possums and others

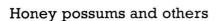

In Australia we can see the partnership taken a step further. A number of tiny pouched mammals (**marsupials**), feed on the nectar produced by *Banksia* and other flowers. Some of them, such as the honey possum have very long, brush-tipped, grooved tongues, suitable for sucking up the abundant nectar. The plants show no special features which might attract these mammals, except that the stamens are long and so spill their pollen easily on to the possum's fine fur.

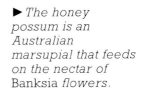

▶ *The honey possum is an Australian marsupial that feeds on the nectar of Banksia flowers.*

◀*Bat-pollinated flowers have all sorts of ways of attracting bats. They make it easy for the bats to get at the nectar, and make sure the bats carry plenty of pollen away with them. The bats possess weak jaws with small teeth. Their tube-like tongues have a tip like a paint brush to help them gather up the nectar.*

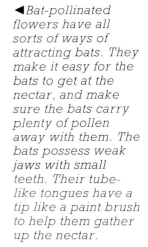

▲ *There are so many features dovetailing the lives of the flowers and the bats that we are sure that their partnership is a very ancient one.*

## A true partnership

Much more important as pollinators are the bats, for they share with insects and birds the ability to move directly between one bloom and the next. About 5 percent of all bat species feed on nectar and pollen. They are all small species that live in warm countries, and most of them are slow flying. Some are capable of hovering like hummingbirds as they feed, but many other bats perch on the flowers, often tearing them with their claws.

Nectar-feeding bats have taken their partnership with plants a stage further than the Australian marsupials. Both the plants and the bats are suited to each other's needs. If either partner becomes endangered, then the other is threatened. The flowers that attract bats are often fairly stoutly built. The ovaries are usually situated below the flowers to protect the developing seeds. The dingy green or purpleish blossoms open at night. They smell strongly and, to our noses, unpleasantly sour or musty. Bat-pollinated flowers are usually well exposed on the outer branches so that they are easy for the bats to reach. They produce a great deal of pollen and a lot of rather sticky nectar. Some bat flowers are bell shaped so that the bats have to push into them, getting showered with pollen. Others are brush-like, with stamens and stigmas arranged so that the bats brush against them as they search for nectar.

# Birds and Seeds

After pollination, a plant sets seeds. The number and size of the seeds vary, but they are generally packaged into a case which is called the **fruit**. Many fruits are large and pulpy and brightly colored and shiny. Their function is not only to protect the seeds, but also to attract animals to eat them.

◀ *Jays and some other birds make winter stores of hard fruit or seeds. They do not always remember where they have stored them.*

▲ *The oilbirds of South America live entirely on fruit and the area around and beneath their nests is a mass of regurgitated seeds. The birds nest deep inside caves where it is pitch dark, so the seeds may germinate, but can never grow.*

Being eaten does not usually destroy the seeds in the fruit. It is part of a partnership in which the animals get moisture, sugars and other nutrients in exchange for taking the seeds away from the parent plants. This is necessary, for the next generation of plants cannot grow up properly too close to their overshadowing elders.

## Carried by birds

When birds eat fruit they sometimes spit out the indigestible seeds some distance away from the parent plant. Sometimes birds swallow the fruits completely so the seeds that they contain are eventually voided with the birds' droppings a long distance from where they were eaten. The seeds come to no harm inside the bird. In many instances, seeds do not germinate unless they have passed through a bird. This is because the seed coat or testa which is strong and protective needs to be weakened in the bird's digestive system before germination can take place.

Some of the most perfect bird–seed partnerships are between the many kinds of mistletoes and the birds that feed on them. In the tropics there are many species of mistletoe which give nectar and fruit to birds. Some of these birds, called mistletoe birds, rely entirely on the mistletoe and, in return, pollinate the plants and spread the seeds.

## Lost larders

Jays have been recorded as making winter larders of acorns several miles away from the tree where the food was collected. They always collect the largest acorns they can carry. Often the acorns are forgotten or lost, and left to grow. Then they will produce trees that, in their turn, have large acorns. Thus jays not only help to spread oak trees, they also influence the type of trees that grow.

►*In Europe, where there is only one kind of mistletoe,* *the mistle thrush feeds on the berries.*

### TIME FOR COURTSHIP

*S*ome large tropical birds may *specialize in feeding on only one kind of fruit. Generally, like the wild avocado, these fruits have a fatty, nutritious rind around a large stone. Such fruits are usually not very noticeable, but the birds that eat them know where they grow and do not need to search hard for them.*

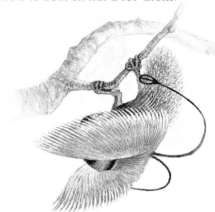

*The beauty and brilliance of some fruit-eaters, such as birds of paradise and the cock of the rock, are linked to their feeding habits. The birds are able to gather their food quickly. The males can then spend much of their time in elaborate courtship displays.*

# Plants and Mammals

In many cases plants produce fruit that appeals to mammals rather than to birds. Such fruit is not brightly colored, but is strongly scented, for mammals that are mainly active at night have poor color vision, but a very good sense of smell. The seeds pass through the animals' digestive system. They germinate well after the seed coat is weakened by the stomach acids.

◄ Through most of the year the trees give squirrels shelter and food. The squirrels "repay" this by spreading the seeds of the trees in the autumn. At this time of year, squirrels gather acorns and other nuts for the winter, but they do not eat them all.

▼ The common hamster gathers seeds and grain in its cheek pouches and may store as much as 198 lbs (90 kg) to see it through the winter.

We can sometimes see an example of this in gardens. Occasionally gardeners use sewage sludge to fertilize their land. If they do this, they sometimes get a large number of unexpected tomato plants. The tomato seeds have survived being eaten by people, and they have then even gone through the sewage treatment system without being damaged!

## Winter stores

Most kinds of rodents store food. The larders of many small mammals consist of a handful of seeds near to their nest. Any seeds left uneaten may germinate and grow, but probably not very well, since they are all buried in one place.

A better partnership exists between trees and squirrels. The squirrels do not remember where they have buried their winter stores but are able to discover the food during the winter because they can smell it in the damp soil. Any nuts that the squirrel does not need or does not find will probably grow, for they have been hidden separately, just as the gardener would plant them. Though animals may seem to eat a lot of nuts, the tree in its hundreds of years of life produces enough for its mammal partners as well as for the growth of new generations of trees.

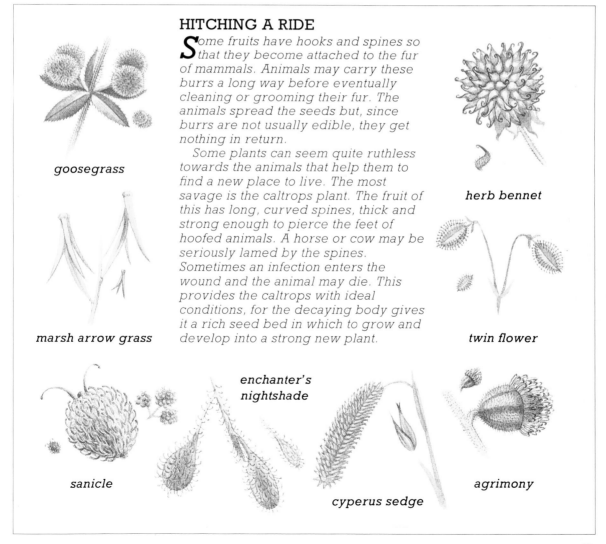

## HITCHING A RIDE

*S*ome fruits have hooks and spines so that they become attached to the fur of mammals. Animals may carry these burrs a long way before eventually cleaning or grooming their fur. The animals spread the seeds but, since burrs are not usually edible, they get nothing in return.

Some plants can seem quite ruthless towards the animals that help them to find a new place to live. The most savage is the caltrops plant. The fruit of this has long, curved spines, thick and strong enough to pierce the feet of hoofed animals. A horse or cow may be seriously lamed by the spines. Sometimes an infection enters the wound and the animal may die. This provides the caltrops with ideal conditions, for the decaying body gives it a rich seed bed in which to grow and develop into a strong new plant.

*goosegrass*

*marsh arrow grass*

*herb bennet*

*twin flower*

*enchanter's nightshade*

*sanicle*

*cyperus sedge*

*agrimony*

# Insects and Seeds

**I**nsects are vital to plants as pollinators and plants "repay" the insects by providing them with food. But insects play little part in spreading the seeds that they helped to create.

One reason for this is that most insect pollinators are short-lived and are nearly all dead by the time the seeds are ripe. Another is that many seeds and fruits are too large and heavy for insects to handle. In spite of this, sweet fruits give sugars to insects, often after the main flowering. They may be important food for honeybees before the cold of autumn sets in.

## Seed-eating ants

Only one group of insects is important in spreading seeds and this is the ants, for certain kinds use seeds as food. They are not very choosy – more than 100 different sorts of seeds have been found in ants'

nests in Europe alone. In dry weather the harvester ants of southern Europe carry and drag small seeds many yards to their nests. A few seeds may be dropped on the way to the nest and these may grow to make more food for the next year. Many American ants with similar habits were at one time said to cultivate the seeds in special gardens, but it is now thought that these are accidental plantings.

▼ *Some of the harvester ants have especially big, powerful heads and jaws. They strip the husk off the seeds before the nutritious part is carried to larders deep underground.*

## Ants and *Codonanthe* vines

The *Codonanthe* vine has special sweet food stores (called extrafloral **nectaries**) at several places on each stem. Ants build small shelters made largely of waste material at each of these points. The plant's roots grow into this nutritious material and the vine thrives for it is getting minerals that are normally scarce for epiphytes. The bigger the vine grows, the more food there is for the ants. As the vine's fruits develop, they also have nectaries and are guarded by the ants. When the seeds are ripe the ants take and plant them in the wall of the nest, which may eventually measure up to 20 inches (50 cm) across.

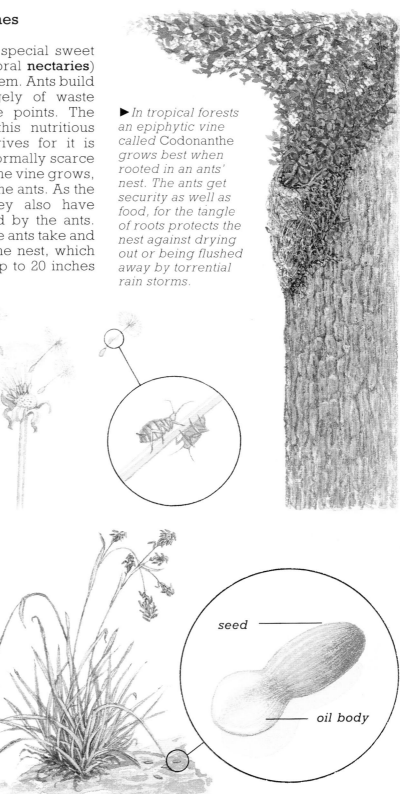

▶*In tropical forests an epiphytic vine called* Codonanthe *grows best when rooted in an ants' nest. The ants get security as well as food, for the tangle of roots protects the nest against drying out or being flushed away by torrential rain storms.*

▶*Seeds may help to spread insects. Winged fruits, like sycamores, or seeds with a parachute of hairs, for example dandelions, may be blown into the air carrying small insects. In this way, creatures such as aphids may colonize remote areas far away from their original home.*

▶*An American sedge* Carex pedunculata *droops its seed heads so that ants can reach them easily. The seeds have oil bodies attached to them. The ants eat these, but then dump the main part of the seeds outside the nest, where they grow. The sedge often grows on rotten tree stumps, where its ant partner lives.*

seed

oil body

# Plant Look-Alikes

**P**lants enlarge the environment for insects, giving them places to rest and hide. Their stems and leaves not only give shelter against bad weather but also against drying out, which is always a danger. Many insects match the color of their background very closely and stand a better chance of survival than those seen easily by their enemies.

◄*Some larger animals imitate plants, like this leaf insect.*

▼ *These insects have evolved to look like their surroundings and their perfect camouflage makes them invisible to their enemies.*

*stick insect*

*leaf insect*

*poplar hawk moth*

*leaf butterfly*

The poplar hawk moth caterpillar, for instance, has stripes like the veins of poplar leaves on its body. It even has little rust-colored patches that are like the color of a common disease of the leaves.

## The best imitators

Even more extreme are some of the stick and leaf insects and the thorn bugs of the tropics. These amazing creatures match their background so exactly that they are quite invisible until they move. The leaf-like praying mantis deceives not only its enemies but also its prey. As it stalks an unwary fly, the mantis quivers like a leaf in the wind, and is not noticed by its victim until it is too late.

## Only leaves?

Some larger animals imitate plants in a general way. But the closest similarities are found among the leaf frogs of South America, and fishes, such as the Amazon leaf fish. This fish is not only colored and shaped like a dead leaf but it floats on its side, so that it *behaves* like one. Its prey do not notice it until they are engulfed by the fish's huge jaws.

Even more extraordinary is the leafy sea dragon. Not a monster, as you might imagine from such a name, but a relative of the sea horses, it lives among the weeds off the coast of Australia, camouflaged by flaps of skin that make it merge totally into its background.

▼ *Flatid bugs from Africa and India have been seen to arrange themselves on a twig, all sitting head uppermost, with greenish colored insects near the top and yellow ones lower down. Together they look like the head of a flower with some buds still unopened – until the whole flower suddenly flies away!*

## PREDATORS BEWARE

*A*lthough in many cases insects help plants, they often cause harm. As a result, plants have slowly changed so that they repel the insects that cause the damage. They have done this by growing leaves that are tough or spiny or hairy or even poisonous so that insects find them impossible or unpleasant to eat.

In some cases, further partnerships have developed. For example, hairy plants sometimes trap insects and some bugs feed on these, managing to avoid the hairs. Occasionally insects are able to overcome the poison. The caterpillars of the cinnabar moth, for instance, feed on the deadly leaves of ragwort, which is eaten by nothing else.

# Insect Protectors

**S**ome sorts of plants are not only pollinated, but also protected by insects. Ants are used for this task. They make excellent guardians for they are active and can bite, sting and squirt acid. They are well able to look after themselves and their home. Also they are long-lived and their colonies survive and defend the plants for many years.

The ant trees of the forests get an extra service from their guardians, for the ants bite off and destroy any creepers or vines that try to get a foothold. Some ants even clean around their particular tree.

## A place of safety

To have a safe place to live seems to be of first importance to the ants. The trees vary in what they offer, but many give easy

◀ *Ants often also keep scale insects which they milk for the sweet honeydew that they produce. The scale insects in the bottom photograph have egg masses.*

▶ *In tropical forests of Africa and South America there are trees like this* Cecropia *which have hollow branches or stems. Ants gnaw through small weak spots and build their nests in the cavities of the branches.*

## HUNTING FOR FOOD PARCELS

*J̶ust as many plants offer nectar to "pay" for pollination, the ant plants produce special food for their "protection gangs." Cecropia trees grow protein-rich swellings at the base of their leaf stems and whistling thorns produce sausage-shaped food parcels at the tips of their leaves. Searching for this food keeps the ants working busily over the branches and leaves. Any other insect will be killed. Even a large animal such as an antelope or monkey that tries to feed on the leaves will be attacked and driven off.*

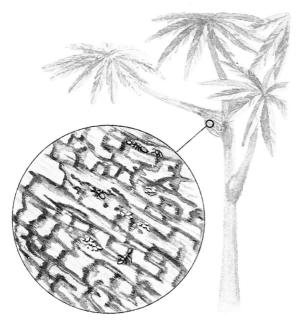

access to a place suitable for a small ant colony. For instance, in some acacias the bases of the huge thorns are soft in their early stages of growth. Ants chew little holes there and excavate the pulpy tissue inside. The outer skin becomes very hard and encloses a good site for a nest.

## Chemical protection

The partnerships between trees and ants must have developed over a very long time, for these specialist ant trees are chemically different from their near relatives. A whistling thorn, for instance, does not have the chemical substances that make other desert acacias unpleasant to eat. Also, if the ants are removed from *Cecropia* trees, the trees are more likely to be attacked by browsing animals.

# Ants, Termites and Fungi

**M**ushrooms and toadstools and other fungi are different from all the rest of the plants in that they can grow in darkness. They are unable to make their own food, but have to rely on the minerals that they get from other plants or animals, living or dead.

Some people think that this difference is so great that the fungi should not be called plants. However, most fungi produce spores and grow very much like other plants, so some botanists include them with the rest of the plant kingdom rather than putting them in their own kingdom.

Some insects use fungi. Some merely eat them, but others, for example wood wasps, cultivate fungi to make food for themselves or their **larvae**. Though they cannot harm people, the females look fearsome for they have long egg-laying tubes (called ovipositors) which look like stings. The ovipositors have sharp saw-like cutting edges and the females use these to make small holes in trees, where they lay their eggs. As they do so, the wasps infect the tree with fungus cells that they carry in little pouches. When the

## A FUNGUS BECOMES A FARMER

*A fungus called* Septobasidium *has a partnership with scale insects which seems almost like science fiction. The fungus grows over the branches of trees, making caverns and tunnels. Scale insects that feed on the sap of the trees live sheltered lives inside the fungus cavities. Some of the insects are normal, and give birth to young in the usual way. But some of the young insects are invaded by the fungus, and the fungus feeds on them. They do not die but continue to grow and even live longer than usual. The fungus in effect farms the insects, and feeds on the trees through them. Many scale insects also form associations with ants.*

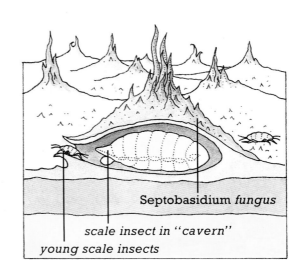

Septobasidium *fungus*

scale insect in "cavern"

young scale insects

wood wasp larvae hatch, they are able to digest the wood that surrounds them, for this has already been changed by the growth of the fungus. Without the fungus the wasps could not feed properly.

## Leaf cutters and fungus gardens

Some kinds of ants, for example leaf-cutters, feed on nothing but fungi. These "gardeners," which live mainly in tropical America, send out hordes of workers which cut leaves from nearby vegetation. The leaves are carried back to the nest, chewed up and made into compost on which the fungus grows.

The ants feed on the growing threads or mycelia of the fungus. When these threads are cut, they often produce small cauliflower-like growths. These are very valuable as food, both for the adult ants and their grubs.

◄*Many kinds of fungi are important because they infect and even kill insects or their caterpillars.*

▼*Some kinds of termites cultivate fungus gardens underground. Though the fungus is grown by many termites, it is not usually important as food. Probably the warmth and moisture made by the growing fungus helps to maintain the right living conditions in the termite hill.*

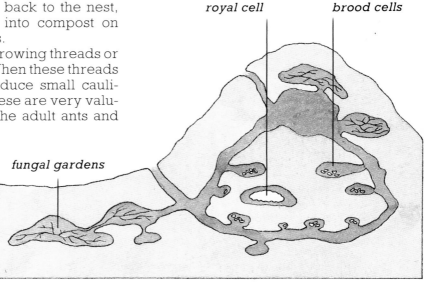

royal cell

brood cells

fungal gardens

# Plant Galls

**I**n summer you can often see strange growths on the leaves and twigs of trees or other plants. These are galls, which are formed by plants when they are invaded by some other organism. Galls may be the result of attack by another plant or fungus, but they are more likely to be the result of an animal's activities.

Galls often occur where mites or insects lay their eggs in a shoot, or a part of the plant that is growing rapidly. The gall gives the grubs food and shelter. At the same time, it keeps them in one place and prevents damage from spreading.

## Insect galls

It is likely that most sorts of galls are part of a very ancient partnership, because each sort of gall-former is generally found on only one kind of plant. Usually each occupies a single type of living place. As a result, a large number of different galls may be found on the same plant, some on the leaves and some on the shoots, for instance. Even different parts of the leaves have their special galls.

Some insects make use of the galls of others and live in them as lodgers. Often these are parasites of the host gall-maker.

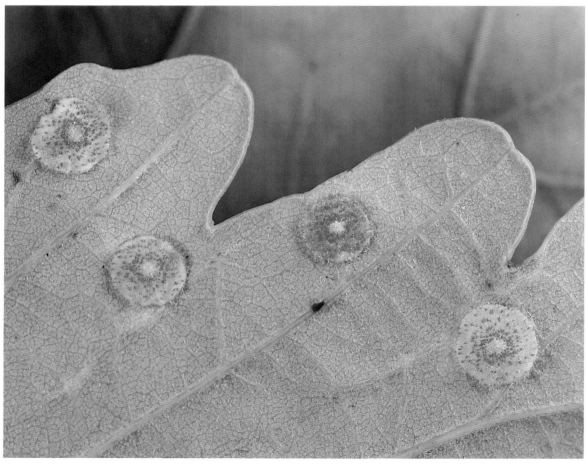

## THE DOUBLE LIFE OF THE OAK APPLE GALL INSECT

*M*any of the gall-forming insects lead a strange double life with two separate generations. The oak apple gall insect is an example of this. In the springtime tiny wasp-like insects climb up the oak trees. They are wingless and they are all females. There are no males in this generation at all. They lay eggs at the base of leaf buds and the area swells to form a spongy ball that looks like a small apple. The grubs inside the oak apples become adults by midsummer.

This second generation has males as well as females and they mate. The females then crawl down the tree and lay eggs in the soil, on the small roots of the tree. Here another sort of gall is formed. After more than a year *wingless females emerge, but no males. They climb up the tree to start the whole circle of life all over again.*

◀*Generally galls do not cause much damage to their hosts. But even a little damage may put a plant at a disadvantage. One way that plants may prevent too much harm is for the galls to be brightly colored or to look like fruit, like this spangle gall. These may attract birds or other animals who will pick off the galls and destroy the insects.*

▼*Animals that cause galls are usually small creatures. Mites, aphids, jumping plant lice, tiny relatives of the wasps and also some beetles, moths and flies may cause galls to form.*

*An aphid gall on hawthorn.*

▼*There are many different shapes and sizes of galls. Some look like fruit, some like tangled fibers. Some measure up to 2 inches (5 cm) across, but others are much smaller.*

*A mite gall on sycamore.*

*A wasp gall, Robins pincushion, on a rose.*

# Flesh-Eating Plants

**O**ne partnership between plants and small animals is particularly unequal. This is the combination of animals and the plants that "eat" them, for few creatures are able to survive the traps laid by flesh-eating plants.

Only about 500 plant species are known to behave in this way. The reason is that they grow in soil so poor that they cannot get enough minerals from it. They overcome this problem by catching and digesting animals and absorbing the nutrients through their leaves.

The butterworts' rosette of leaves attracts small flies and ground-living creatures. The leaf's sticky surface holds them and special cells exude a liquid to kill and digest them. While this is happening, the leaves roll inwards, but they flatten again once their job is done.

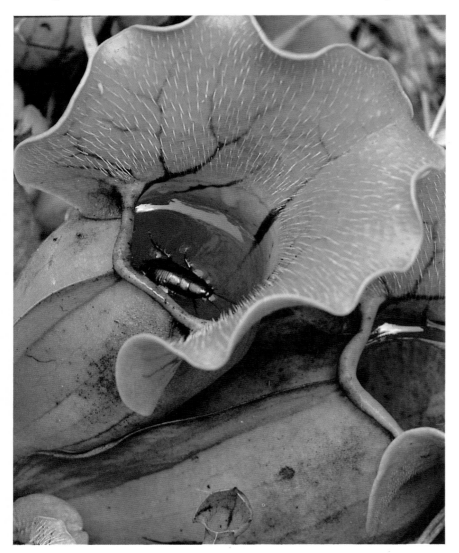

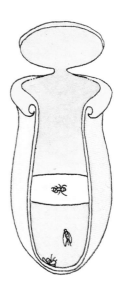

◀Pitcher plants have urn-shaped leaves that contain liquid. Insects are attracted by the color and smell. They fall in and cannot escape for their prison has slippery walls and is barred by hairs.

The leaves of sundews carry long hairs, each crowned with a drop of glue. Insects looking for a meal get stuck on the glue. More and more hairs bend over them making escape impossible. It takes several days for the insect to be digested. After this the hairs straighten and dry, so that any hard parts left unused fall off and are blown away.

## Traps and nooses

Hairs are also important to the Venus's fly-trap. They are triggers which, when touched twice by an insect, cause the leaf cage to snap shut.

A hair also triggers the action of the bladderwort. When it is touched by an animal such as a water flea, it causes the lid of the trap to fly open. Water gushes in carrying the creature with it. When the water pressure is the same inside and outside the trap, the lid closes. Strangest of all are the soil fungi which, when they come into contact with an eelworm, throw a noose of cells about it. From these they absorb the tissues of their prey.

## Pitcher robbers

Some creatures take advantage of the carnivorous plants. A few flies and caterpillars have feet capable of climbing up the waxy inner walls of pitcher plants and they prey on the captive insects. Some spiders spin webs across the mouth of the pitcher, to take first choice of the catch. One of these spiders is resistant to the digestive juices of the plant, should it happen to fall in.

◀Sundews have flowers that are long-stemmed and short-lived. They are only for attracting insect pollinators. The flowers never kill their visitors. They look very different from and grow as far away from the insect-trapping leaves (shown here) as possible.

▶ The traps are always formed from the leaves. Some, like the sundews and butterworts, make simple "fly paper" traps. The pitcher plants make pitfall traps. The Venus's flytrap makes a spring trap, while the bladderwort uses a vacuum trap. In the soil there are tiny fungi that snare and lasso eelworms. Plants only eat small creatures – there are no man-eating plants!

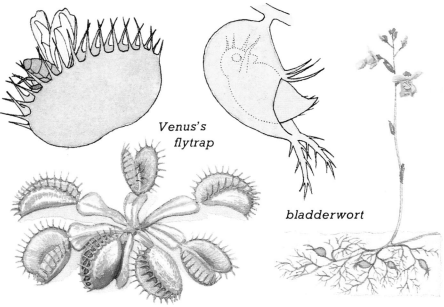

Venus's flytrap

bladderwort

# Useful Plants

Like all other animals, human beings make use of plants for the oxygen that they produce, and for food. But we use plants in many other ways. Our earliest ancestors may have picked up a piece of wood to knock down some fruit that was out of reach or to kill an animal for food. At a later time branches may have been dragged together to make a shelter, perhaps thatched with grass.

We share the making of simple tools with our close relatives the great apes, and the use of plants for shelter and bedding with many creatures that make nests. But at this point we leave the rest of the animals behind, for human beings use plants for many other purposes.

## The discovery of fire

One of the first and most important was the discovery that dry grass and wood would burn. Fire enabled people to keep themselves warm, to frighten away wild animals, to light their living area and, most valuable of all, to cook their food. Cooking meant that early communities could use new sorts of food that might not have been edible raw, so the danger of starvation was pushed back a bit. At a later time, fire was the major weapon used to trap large numbers of animals. In some places it is still used to clear forests and other areas wanted for growing crops.

◄In prehistoric times, people used the plants that grew around them, taking what they needed from the wild. In many parts of the world this still happens.

►Wherever humans take their crops, weed seeds also go. Sometimes weeds grow much better in their new surroundings and become a serious nuisance. It is as if the plant world is getting back at humans for their exploitation of nature.

## The beginning of agriculture

About 10,000 years ago a great change occurred. It was discovered that seeds thrown on to the ground would grow, so it was not necessary to travel to where choice plants lived – they could be brought to the human settlements. Plants began to be cultivated, and people always selected seeds from the biggest and strongest plants. In the end they looked quite different from their wild ancestors.

## Spread by trade

In more recent times, as new continents were discovered, old crops were taken to the new worlds and new crops were brought back by the travelers. Nowadays we tend to forget that the potato came first from the Andes, or that oranges, grown in most warm countries, originated in China. Even a garden or a park will contain flowers from many parts of the world.

 *► People use some plants for food or medicines. Some are used for fibers, ropes or cloth, or in the construction of huts and shelters. Others are made into brightly colored dyes, or grown for their beauty and the pleasure they give.*

*Wheat is used to make flour for bread and cakes*

*Hardwoods are used to make furniture*

*Plants like woad are used to dye cloth*

*Some plants like foxglove are used to make medicines*

*Cotton fibers can be spun and woven into cloth*

# Plants into the Future

In many ways people still treat the world as our ancient ancestors did. They use the natural resources of animals and plants as though these were endless and there would always be more. We now know that this is not so. Our spherical earth is finite and our partnership with living things must be more than mere exploitation.

In spite of knowing the dangers, in many areas the Stone-Age type of destruction goes on. Rain forests, which were once thought to be inexhaustible, are now being felled at such a rate that they will be totally destroyed by the end of the century if nothing is done to save them. Other places have lost all their plants because farmers have tried to grow crops to feed the increasing numbers of people. It is said that there is nearly as much desert caused by human misuse as there is well-farmed land.

## Science and plants

In the last 20 years a new partnership has grown up between plants and humans. Scientists have discovered new ways of growing crops, and have developed new strains of plants which ripen more quickly and are more resistant to pests and diseases. Genetic engineering has shown that in the laboratory it is possible to alter the basic structure of plants, and make them more suitable to human needs.

## Our future world

Where in all this do the plants benefit from the partnership? It is difficult to see. A few species may be greatly increased in numbers, but it is likely that many others will be completely destroyed. We have been slow in coming to realize the value of the variety of plants that share the world with us. The more we destroy, the less we shall have to enjoy, and the less variety there will be to improve the world of the future.

◀ *We, in our spaceship earth, need to remain on good terms with our plant partners, not only for their benefit but also for ours.*

▶ *In some areas as here in Ontario, replanting replaces trees removed by logging. But trees form only a part of the habitat. Without the other plants and animals that have been lost, the forest is not the same.*

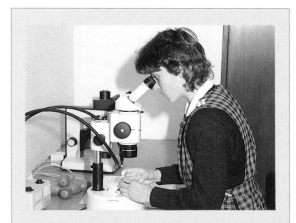

## NEW PLANTS FOR FOOD AND INDUSTRY

*S*cientists have also been exploring the possibilities of new crop plants. Grass-like plants that live in the edge of the sea could provide animal fodder and even grain. Desert plants, capable of surviving with very little water could be cultivated. In the future we may see many new foods on the supermarket shelves. Also, single-celled plants may be processed to make food for us and for farm animals.

Other plants may be found for industrial purposes. One desert plant, the Jojoba, produces an oil which can be used for lubrication purposes that used to call for whale oil. There may well be others.

# Glossary

**Algae** (*singular alga*) Flowerless plants, always found in water or damp places. Some, including the seaweeds, are large but most consist of a single cell and can only be seen through a microscope.

**Anther** The part of the stamen of a flowering plant in which pollen forms.

**Bract** A small, simply shaped leaf, formed at the base of a flower stem.

**Calyx** The outer part of a flower. It usually consists of green leaf-like sepals, which protect the flower bud.

**Canopy** The level of the upper branches in a forest.

**Chlorophyll** The green pigment of plants that absorbs energy from sunlight to make food by photosynthesis.

**Club mosses** Non-flowering plants that produce spores, like ferns. In the past many club mosses grew to the size of large trees. Today, they are all small.

**Crown** The upper and outer branches of a tree, which give it its shape.

**Epiphyte** A plant that grows on another plant, taking only support and light but not nourishment.

**Fern** A spore-producing, non-flowering plant, often with complex leaves.

**Fruit** The part of a plant that carries the ripe seeds. It may be brightly colored or sweet tasting to attract animals, which will spread the seeds. Some are plumed so that the wind carries the seeds.

**Fungus** (*plural fungi*) Simple spore-producing plants including mushrooms, molds and yeasts. Unlike all other plants they do not make their own food, but take what they need from other plants or animals, living or dead.

**Gall** An abnormal growth on a plant caused when insects, mites or fungi damage a fast growing area.

**Germination** The beginning of growth of a seed or a spore.

**Habitat** The place where a plant or animal lives.

**Haustorium** (*plural haustoria*) A root-like part of a parasitic plant that invades its host and takes food from it.

**Honey guides** Lines or blotches of intense color towards the center of a flower. They attact pollinating insects towards a reward of nectar.

**Host** A plant or an animal that gives support, protection and food to an individual of another species (a parasite), but gets nothing in return.

**Humus** Dead plant and animal remains, broken down in the soil.

**Larva** (*plural larvae*) The early stage of life of many animals without backbones, also fishes and amphibians. Caterpillars and grubs are larvae, so are tadpoles.

**Lichens** A group of non-flowering plants. Each lichen is a mixture of algal and fungal cells, but is bigger and different from either of the partners that go to make it up.

**Liverworts** Small, creeping non-flowering plants, which are usually found in damp places. They are related to mosses.

**Marsupial** A mammal in which the young are born in a very undeveloped state but are then nourished in a pouch on the belly of their mother. They are sometimes called "pouched mammals".

**Minerals** The non-living chemical materials of which rocks and part of the soil are formed.

**Mosses** Small non-flowering plants usually found in damp places. They are like liverworts, but generally have upright stems.

**Mycorrhiza** A fungus that grows on or in the roots of many kinds of plants, providing them with certain nutrients.

**Nectar** A sugary fluid produced by many kinds of flowers. It is an important food for pollinating insects.

**Nectary** The gland in a flower in which nectar is formed. A few plants produce nectar on the stems or leaves in extra-floral nectaries.

**Nutrient** Nourishment or food.

**Ovary** In plants, the part of the flower in which the seeds develop.

**Parasite** A plant or an animal that lives on or inside another (its host), taking food, support and shelter, but giving nothing in return.

**Photosynthesis** The process by which green plants build up sugars and starches. They take water and minerals from the soil, carbon dioxide gas from the air and use the sun's energy as fuel for this activity.

**Pollen** Tiny grains that contain the male sex cells of conifers and flowering plants.

**Pollination** The transfer of pollen from the male anther to the female stigma of a flower of the same species. The male and female cells fuse to form a seed.

**Pollinator** An animal, usually an insect, but sometimes a bird or a mammal, that carries pollen from one flower to another, so that pollination may take place.

**Pollinium** *(plural pollinia)* The pollen masses produced by orchids, which are stuck to the bodies of pollinators.

**Prey** Animals, usually plant eaters, which are the food of flesh eaters. For instance, mice are the prey of owls and cats, antelopes are the prey of hyaenas and lions.

**Saprophyte** A plant able to break down the tissues of dead plants and animals and use them as food. Saprophytes do not need to photosynthesize and often live in shadowy places, such as deep woodland.

**Self-pollination** The transfer of pollen from the male part to the female part of a flower on the same plant.

**Soredia** Reproductive organs of lichens.

**Spores** Tiny reproductive particles formed by plants. Non-flowering plants (ferns, mosses etc), produce huge numbers of spores. When these germinate, they grow into an intermediate plant, known as the gametophyte generation.

**Stamen** The part of a flower that produces pollen. It consists of a stalk or filament and an anther, in which the pollen grows.

**Starch** A substance formed from sugars in plants. It is usually stored in the roots or seeds and is changed back into sugar when the plant needs it for growth.

**Stigma** The top of the style in a flower. It is sticky and pollen that lands on it is held there so that pollination can take place.

**Style** An outgrowth from the female part of a flower. The style pushes the stigma into a position in which it can catch pollen brought by pollinators.

**Sugar** Sugars are made by plants through photosynthesis. They enable the plants to grow and are a source of energy for animals that eat them.

**Symbiosis** Two different sorts of organisms living together. They may be two plants, two animals or a plant and an animal. Each helps the other, and in some cases it is impossible for either to survive without its partner.

**Xylem** The woody tissues of plants that carry water and minerals from the roots to the rest of the plant.

**Zooxanthellae** Minute plants that live symbiotically in the tissues of corals and many other simple animals.

# Index

# Further Reading

## Young Adult Books – General

Black, David. *Plants*. New York: Facts On File, 1986.

Forsthoeful, John. *Discovering Botany*. New York: DOK Publishers, 1982.

Lambert, David. *Vegetation*. New York: Franklin Watts, 1984.

## Young Adult Books – Plant Partnerships

Bender, Lionel. *Plants*. New York: Franklin Watts, 1988.

Conway, Lorraine. *Plants*. Good Apple, 1980.

## Adult Books – General Reference about Botany

New England Wild Flower Society Staff. *Botany for All Ages*. New Jersey: Globe Pequot Press, 1989.

Rost, Thomas L. Botany: *A Brief Introduction to Plant Biology*. New York: John Willey & Sons, 1984.

Tootill, Elizabeth (ed.). *The Facts On File Dictionary of Botany*. New York: Facts On File, 1984.

## Adult Books – Plant Partnerships

Scott, Jane. *Botany in the Field: An Introduction to Plant Communities for the Amateur Naturalist*. New York: Prentice Hall, 1984.

---

## Photographic credits

*t* = top, *b* = bottom, *l* = left, *r* = right

Cover: Bruce Coleman/B and C Calhoun; page 6 Bruce Coleman/Hans Reinhard; page 7*t* Frank Lane/Peggy Heard; page 7*b* Bruce Coleman/Gerard Cubitt; page 8 Bruce Coleman/Alain Compost; page 10 Bruce Coleman/Adrian Davies; page 11 Bruce Coleman/Gerard Cubitt; page 12 Bruce Coleman/Charlie Ott; page 13 Bruce Coleman/M.P.L. Fogden; page 14*t* Bruce Coleman/F. Merçay; page 14*b* Bruce Coleman/Charlie Ott; page 15*t* Bruce Coleman/Alain Compost; page 15*b* Bruce Coleman/Adrian Davies; page 16 Bruce Coleman/Hans Reinhard; page 18 Frank Lane/M. Thomas; page 19*l* Bruce Coleman/A. Davies; page 19*r* Bruce Coleman/Charlie Ott; page 20 Bruce Coleman/Carl Roessler; page 21 L. Pitkin; page 22 L. Pitkin; page 24 Frank Lane/Leo Batten; page 26*t* Frank Lane/W.T. Davidson; page 26*b* Frank Lane/L. West; page 27 J. Pope; page 28 Bruce Coleman/L.C. Marigo; page 29*t* Bruce Coleman/M. Timothy O'Keefe; page 29*b* Frank Lane/K.G. Preston-Mafham; page 30 Frank Lane/J. Hutchings; page 31 Bruce Coleman/Hans Reinhard; page 32 Harry Smith; page 33 Bruce Coleman/J. Anthony; page 34 Bruce Coleman/W. Lankinen; page 37 Bruce Coleman/J. Taylor; page 38 Frank Lane/Silvestris; page 39 Bruce Coleman/Hans Reinhard; page 40*l* Frank Lane/J. Watkins; page 40*r* Frank Lane/Hans Dieter; page 42 Bruce Coleman/Jeff Foot; page 44 Bruce Coleman/Gerard Cubitt; page 45 Bruce Coleman/Eric Crichton; page 46*t* Frank Lane/K.G. Preston-Mafham; page 46*b* Frank Lane/K.G. Preston-Mafham; page 47 Frank Lane; page 48 Bruce Coleman/Peter Ward; page 50 Bruce Coleman/Neville Fox-Davies; page 51 J. Pope; page 52 Bruce Coleman/L.L. Rue III; page 53 Frank Lane/M.B. Withers; page 54 Bruce Coleman/L.C. Marigo; page 55 Frank Lane/M.J. Thomas; page 56 Bruce Coleman/NASA; page 57*t* Bruce Coleman/J. Fennell; page 57*b* Bruce Coleman/S. Kaufman.